THE WALLOWED CAROUSEL

A WORDLESS POETRY

SUHAIL SHAGUL HAMEED

"Dedicated to the Young Adults, War Veterans, and

everyone who fights a battle within themselves"

Contents

Contents

Foreword

I'd like to express my heartfelt gratitude to my Family, Friends, my esteemed mentors ;

Dr. M Shanmugam (Neurosurgeon), Dr. G Egambaram (M.O.T(Paediatrics)), Dr. S. Arun (B.O.T), Dr. M Mahendran (BOTh, MFA, DCA, MOTh(Paediatrics), II-DAN), Dr. Sindhu. S (B.O.T), Pargavi. R (MSc. Psychology), Dr. Rajesh Y (MPT Neuro), Dr. Barani Gnanasekaran (MBBS), and Dr. S Abhinesh (MBBS) in aiding me with the completion of this book.

Thank you for granting me your precious time and encouragement, which has enabled me to launch this book.

Preface

Reading this amazing book named *Talking with Psychopaths and Savages, a work by Christopher Berry-Dee*, and *The Textbook of Personality Disorders by Andrew E Skodol & John M Oldham*, and *American Psycho by Bret Easton Ellis* and also the works of my two favorite psychologists, *Sigmund Freud and Carl Jung*, and the cinematic portrayal of psychiatric disorders and being able to learn about them, and read about the research works related to them, (I'd like to mention the National Library of Medicine here), inspired me to write this collection of poetry dedicated to those that are unable to express themselves.

I had always been intrigued by learning about them and finding out the ways of treatment in various realms of Occupational Therapy, Medicine, Rehabilitation teams, etc, and the methods incorporated in aiding those that have been affected psychologically in being able to survive in this beautiful world of harmony and diversity.

I started this work in October of 2021 and completed it as recently as December 5th, 2023. It has been quite a journey, I indulged myself in. My deep gratitude to you for selecting to acquire this book, and providing me with your support.

To quote un quote by Mrs. Michelle Obama,

""At the root of this dilemma is the way we view mental health in this country. Whether an illness affects your heart, your leg or your brain, it's still an illness, and there should be no distinction ""

Prologue

Sometimes, psychiatric conditions and issues may be viewed as a taboo, eerie, or horrifying topic, because of the way they are portrayed like that in the big and small screens our brains collect information from. Yeah, the dark side and negative effects appear scary, but have we ever thought of the struggles they face? Every second, every minute, every hour, every day, chained up like dogs and treated like scum. Yes, we cannot co-exist with them in the same world together, because we are far too complex for them to perceive and understand us. What I'm trying to put front is not the fact that we need to treat them the way we treat our usual mates, they are just a different kind of humans, a little closer to the animal kingdom than us. Tell me, how many animals fear them? And how most of them are with most animals? We choose the vibes to be around us, those that we can relate to, and so do they. But what I'm rather trying to say is, that all we can do is, guide them on to the kind of their world, or to places where their needs will be mustered. Would you leave a hurt or wounded kitten or a puppy to rot on the roadside, just because it's noisy and seems aggressive? No.

But what's also important, is that we do what is best for them and we have to make sure and be aware that we are not hurt or damaged in the process.

Those that we call "mentally or psychologically ill" appear to be closer to being true homo sapiens than most of us, that sometimes hide behind masks and disguises, and add dirt to our heart and put up a show, and hide our intrusiveness, and cherish all lies, and find disgust and discomfort in the truth, we tend to flee far from it.

Follow me and dive into my mind, as I explore some of the many conditions we have heard of or faced a breeze of it at some point in our lifetime.

So, Welcome to The Wallowed Carousel!

Acknowledgements

Thank you Lord Almighty for blossoming these thoughts and ideas in me
and enabling me to complete this beautiful work.
If it were'nt for You, I'd be nothing.
Shukran ya Rabb.

A Tiny Tip

Make sure to read the first letters of the lines in (some poems) to find out the POV of that prose.

1. A ROSY TALE - 1

"*What is the relationship between a Man and a Woman? It has been around since the beginning of time, and almost everything revolves around it. Hold my hands, and let me guide you through this melodious ride, where I present its nectar, in a way I have used the colors.*"

THE BEGINNING

The bond between a male and a female,

Man and Woman, Boy and girl,

Masc or Fem, and other terms associated,

Is poetically exquisite, in its way.

It's the woeful emotions and feelings,

Those influential toxic factors,

That tarnish the beauty of this connection so sublime.

The bond is synonymous with the enticing, elegant, and vibrantly radiant rose,

With its green majestic stalk,

That wields their unsheathed swords.

The boy, man, male, or masc,

Relates the thorns, that prick,

Yet handsome and tough,

Protecting the fortress,

From predators and hunters,

The tough, rough, mighty,

Loyal, protective, and gusty,

Enwraps the beautifully adorned flower,

The eye of attraction and tempting seduction,

The ravishing, tranquil, and harmonical component,

That decors the thorns and grants them peace,

From battles and offer comfort,

And embrace them with her calming aura,

And enclose them with on, with a whisper.

2. MASQUERADE

"What if your loved ones weren't actually them, but someone else impersonating them? That'll be one hell of a ride, won't it ? Sooo, Buckle up for some Suspicion."

Calling out my dear ones,

Appeared before me all at once,

Pipe down all my senses,

Glancing at them, I say,

Replaced have they been,

Aliens, robots, or some demonic kin,

Supernatural or a fathomless tin?

Say, do you know who is who,

Yeet them out, this ain't my lil bro,

Nothing you say shall fool a crow,

Deep down, I know, with you I did not grow,

Repeat the façade and all this charade,

Over the days, I shall sing this ballad,

Mother, father, brother, and dear old sister,

Eyes mine see and ears hear aloud,

I perceive very well, almost so clear,

I am Sherlock in flesh, so be aware,

But, you babe, too aren't my known lovely dear,

You are someone a stranger,

A Masquerading danger.

3. FLICK MAGIC

"Stealing something or anything for no apparent reason, we've seen many do it and most of us have been through it while growing up, but this ride's going to be a hysterical one."

Kick the bucket? Nah, I'd flick it Tho,

Loreal Paris, no need, still pick it go,

Emporio, I own with no nickel given,

Pocket stuff, I'd never use, even sour pickles,

Tempted to grab random things in a trickle,

Oh dear, oh god, I even loot my lil brother's suckle,

Tell me why can't I stop this jiggle?

Mayhem all around might even steal some rubble,

Arms and hands, pick stuff I'd never nibble,

Not on a plan, I don't know why,

I keep doing this dribble,

I aint no thief, don't put me w em as a couple,

All tries in pure vain, should I make hand dismantle?

Should I call for help? Or should I let time take the handle?

4. YOU CRAVE ME

"Ever came across those persistent "lovers" who believe you are in love with them when you don't even know them? Come forth this ride, that I call Errroto,"

Elixirs on her table, that's her secret,

Rusted clips, beneath her closet,

On the road, she rides a teal black scooter,

Tea no milk, sugar cubes and colder,

Off road café, n an occasional smoker,

Maple leaf, where she works as doctor,

All fit club, she lifts to be toner,

Night colds in, she feels hotter,

I know, me is the one, on her thoughts run harder,

Across the streets, she stands by the roadside,

I know real well, that she wants me beside and close,

Her wish is for me, to be Her's forever,

I watch all hours, like her carer,

Can't see me, I hide blender,

She won't say, but I know the cluster,

Of her feelings and her emotional buster,

She'll never tell me, she desires my touch over,

But I do know, in her heart, she craves,

Me be her lover.

So, I watch over her, and invaginate her trail,

Cuz, I perceive well, and I believe,
She's obsessed over me and me she craves,
She won't show, but I know what's in her case.

5. A ROSY TALE - 2

THE ESSENCE

In a way, the mothers soothe their infants,

'It's fine to lay low, feel some rest,

You needn't be fighting, for the rest.

You have my lap and my shoulders,

I shall tend and improve,

That what you protect so pure.

So despair not,

Your struggles are never in vain'

Like a breeze that brushes past your skin barren,

And the kind that your dry lips wetten therein.

Synonymous with the sun's rays,

When it moves into a haze,

Words that resonate love,

Care, affection, and peaceful snow.

Focal from her heart, beneath it,

Words that carry the power to enwrap,

Replenish the blemish,

And Heal the scars,

And instills a peaceful sedation in her arms.

"The man enwraps the female, the woman enwraps the male, it is bond of interconnection without any junction"

6. OSCILLATIONS

"You are in for a ride where extremes is the only pattern, you are either on the peak or at the bottom, there's no in between, So Buckle up to Oscillaaate!"

Bright up the lights, let the fun flow,

I am above the clouds, catch me float,

Party like hell, there is no drought,

Open the doors, here I come,

Lavish and ravish, watch me Mom,

Adrenaline Pump, power-filled morn,

Raging through the darkness, watch em crumb.

Disturbing lights, turn em down,

I am feeling crap, halt the dumb,

Synthetic drugs, between my thumb,

Open my mouth, pills on my tongue,

Reverse all hours, hit on a bong,

Destined to be a loner, trunk let hang?

Enwrapped and tangled in a sadness song,

Rusty veins, feel my end bells clang,

On top of the world at times, pridely proud,

Wanna be dead, still wrapped and shroud,

Break a breath, when I see and hear em,

Others don't see or feel, they call it hallustuff,

Maybe, I think, I should slit with a toughened tuft.

7. SUICIDE BY THE SEA

"A final note, my dear friend left before he decided to conclude his
story.…leading to his final moments,..
Bear with me, for this slow and heartbreaking ride.…"

I stand by the chilly cold sea,

The salty water on my feet, spree.

Ah! The moon is so bright and full of glee.

Lovely is the night, with its trees,

Lonely is my story, like that of fleas,

Towards you, my thoughts they steer,

Yearning for you, although you sneer.

Time moves by, the days I fear,

Whispers and hatred, my heart it hears.

Too far, but yet so near,

Hold me in your arms, my lovely dear,

Ah! Did I ever tell you how me feel? (in your vicinity)

Beautiful is you, as the humid morning dew,

Rageful voices amidst my demonic crew,

Vices of lust lost from love,

But , I see you, this is the trance of love,

Look at me, I'm a lonely dove,

Into the sea, I shift and drove,

Open-armed, into the abyss I dove,

Memories of us, before I wry,

Wish I could let it all out and cry,
Bu- e Gu- ss tha-s e',
Gulp *Burp* *Burp*
That was my weak soul's, last breath gone dry.

8. TACHYCARDIA - 1

"Ever felt your heart going on a ride, and your stomach on Euphoria, when you are captivated by that one? That's pleasurably painful yeah? Come on over, mi amor, for this ride, its going to be melancholic and ravishing, this evening shall we melt, so there's no need to buckle up, just hold my hand tight yet gentle."

MOMENTS BEFORE TACHYCARDIA

Sun rays through my window pain,
Sweet flower-scented meadow train,
A feast for eyes, that glance in a chain,
Inhale a breath, trance of rain,
So is your visage, so tranquil and saint,
Eyes that move so beautifully taint,
Stuns my heart, a soulful giant,
Lost In your beauty, a void so pretty,
Ravish and lovely, lavishly setting,
Amidst the minds that run crafty,
I met you, a lovable poetry.
Gaze so intense makes my blood highly tense,
Wish I could talk, but I've lost all sense,
Smile so sharp, you make me gasp,
Arms that embrace and fingers that grasp

9. TACHYCARDIA - 2

120 BPM
Guide me and lead me,
Chide me and devour me,
See you and see me,
You are the one, that free set me,
I engrave words, I fail to articulate,
My lips too numb, so a poem I create,
There are more I'd love to say,
Merge, admire, adore, a crave to faze,
I shall preserve it for the moment you shall say,
For the sparks of love and bond of soul,
I yearn for the day our hands shall hold,
To preserve an eternal love, with the
Lustre like that of gold.

10. THE MOMENT

"*Let's take a break and pause in Cupid's Park for a while. Read through and envision what your eyes see, close the eyelids and feel the presence.*"

Under the setting sun,

The rays scatter,

Glistening everything it playfully touches.

From the grass to the roads,

To the trees, to the shores,

To the free birds that return after a long day's haul.

Bright red flowers, adorn the pavement,

Aesthetic tulips bordering the corners,

Lavenders spread out, a treat for eyes,

Roses, hibiscus, jasmine, and the stargazer lily.

All assembled and placed with dahlias amidst.

We sat within the Iris to our right,

The Daises on our left,

The Daffodils to our south,

The Lantanas to our north,

Benesth us lay, the Lavenders and Poppies,

Enclosing us is the Helianthus Annuus,

The flower close to your heart.

Les Moments coulent,

A chill breeze hugs us both,

Bringing forth butterflies and pretty Moths.

The Sun melts,

Blending with the night,

Creating the dusk,

Orange, Red, Yellow, Purple, Green,

And your presence.

The colors sing of love,

And the scenery hums romance.

The raindrops drip,

Upon our skin,

The chilly sensation, yet humid,

The lunar peeks from the curtain of the tranquil night,

The sounds of the waterfalls, cease,

They flow gentle, in reverence to the melting sun,

The tune of Peace and Calmness, reverberate,

This moment with you,

Dolce Far Niente, Ou...

A slow deep breath inhaled,

The fragrance stimulates the Bulb Olfactory,

Dopamine release,

Serotonin flows,

A potion is created,

With a touch of Oxytocin and some Vasopressin dose.

The Fingers sense the soft wet grass,

And brushing the hair strands that block the view,

Lips smile sharp yet relaxed,

In this moment,

Think of nothing but Sense everything,

The wind on the feet,

The heat on the back,

The chillness on the warm hands,

The warmth in the lips,

The relaxed Eyes,

And the nose at rest,

The ear and nature,

In a feast aforementioned.

The scenery doesn't end here,

I want you to describe your presp,

And see the world through your lens,

Tell me, mon couer,

What makes nature so pretty?

11. MOMENTS BY YOU

"This page is your canvas, as a memoir, we leave in places we visit, I want you to write of your Dream land or of a Moment or Love or any shall it be, Engrave herein your words, those that stay close to your heart, Listen to YOU and let the ink caress the paper below."

12. ROLLER-COASTER - 1

*"Y'Know what's Schizo? Well, it is someone wh- ou ou, No Spoilers,
Warning : This ride only for the daring hearts.
Hop on this Mind and Vestibular Blowing Rollercoaster, you are in
for some reckless ride!"*

THE RISE

See over to the corner, a man there stands,

Call me crazy, my eyes see what ye don't,

Hate on me, for my weird capabilities,

I know well, I'm psychotic and full of abilities,

Zip up my dreams, fear of every possibility,

On the pretty road brightness, I see harmful disruptiveness,

Pass into night's sleep, creeping paranoia upon,

Me dorm enwrapped in darkness.

13. ROLLER-COASTER - 2

THE FALL

Help! I scream and I cry, please, expel these visions,

Rage-filled souls what are these emotions?

Enthralled was me, I'm loved said they,

Not to mention all thought I was dead insane,

In this small world, present on the lane, yet not,

All fun ways to end my poem, gnaw at my toes and cot,

Hoping I'd slit my throat and right into a grave, toss and caught,

Elicit flowers of anger and anxious thorns,

Lessen my voice and thoughts and yawn,

People suck, to meself I talk,

Many demons under my bed, with blades they stalk,

Elixir absent, quite the novelic comical hell,

Tell me, will I ever be cured, or remain diabolical?

14. CLEAVE ART

"Ever heard of those that have the urge to sever their own limbs and parts? Welcome to the Haunted Ride, stiffen up your hearts and buckle up your stomach, if You know what I mean!"

Arms soft and thighs so tender,

Pleasurably would I let them asunder,

Obsidian sword, obrez, or an obliterator,

The options are wide, call me self-amputator,

Ethereal it may be, wanna put my hand into a blender,

Maintain the hold, feel the blades on my tendon,

Nifty and swiftly, it's an art to be praised,

Over and over, these people call me craze,

Ponder envisioned, even you'd be fazed,

Have you cut your arm? A finger or toe?

Ever seen your flesh and blood? A fountain of two?

Lovingly, enticingly do I crave,

Intriguing is the desire, to slice and clave,

Ask me to you, why am I in this cave?

Locked up in shackles, like a madman's dame

15. LEUCINE - 1

"Ever heard of those that can't express or feel any emotion at all? And those that can cry no more? Lace up, for some static ride....."

Lucky are those who can cry,
Whenever they feel so dry,
Do they eyes pain, when filled with tears?
Or does the heart lighten from the ache?
Do you run out of breath?
Or do you gain back your soul, away from death?
Do the tears, purify your face?
Or do they heal what's hidden, under the chase?
Tell me, does the heart still feel?
Any kind of emotional peels.

16. LEUCINE - 2

• 21 •

A TALK OF FEELINGS

How is it to be on a rollercoaster?

To be able to feel something and muster it.

Do they forth come the warm tears?

Or do they float you and make you smile so dear?

Or do they make your face a bit frownier?

Or does it help you laugh with people and act clownier?

Lucky are those, who can feel,

Some kind of sentimental meal,

And shed em tears, when they want,

Relieving their burden by dawn,

Healing scars of untold thorns,

So tell me, my friend, with the horns,

Are the tears still warm?

Or is it just a Colden charm?

17. VOID OF DARKNESS - 1

"We all have been at rock bottom, haven't we? Accompany me on this ride, as we sink deep down the abyss.."

Drowning in the abyss of darkness,

Embark on my journey of eternal dampness.

Prescriptions crumble, like towers n dungeons,

Ride through the rigid shadows and pungent.

Ethanol causes damage, might I should try,

Slit my throat and veins, pull the lot, and dry,

Scared of the light, I'm left to rot and cry.

In my realm, hope all they halt,

Open me chambers, never good enough.

Night crawls and gnaws, close the casket

Let me sign off,

Will I be loved? Taken? Cared? Or chosen?

Crouch me in a corner, all days darken,

Rhythm of hellish bells, is heaven hotter?

Leap off a cliff, let me bones clatter.

Hush lil human, don't be a monster,

Lesser do they know, the scars burn castor,

Aight, lets shush the noises and pull out the voices.

18. SHHHHH, BEWARE

"Ever been shit scared of every aspect of everything?

- WARNING : This ride causes Insomnia -"

Put out the lights, they might find me,

Across the realms and fateful decree,

Rustling leaves, did me they see?

Air through the keyhole, make no breathe,

Night falls in, the evils shall rise,

Out for me, they chase all light,

Ignite no fires, I'd rather freeze,

All Do not let see me, even family smiles in glee,

Disturbed water, think I should flee,

It is someone, creasing the pathway behind that tree,

Sound of some birds, it might be a spy,

Over me, they hover, over and over,

Run should me, for me dark cover,

Deep beneath the ocean,

Escape amidst the drunken,

Ransack my house, you find nothing,

Except for stupid papers or silly writings,

Burn them, I should, or they'll track me,

The tap runs flow, someone's inside the hole,

Wind rustles, who gushes forth?

North, south, west, or east?

Up, down, left or right,
I'm dead scared and petrified,
What is going to happen,
Why do I fear?
Why did that happen,
That has left me this stricken.
(I need to pack up myself tight)

19. VOID OF DARKNESS - 2

My mind is full of dark red vices,

Would you be my friend until the end of gases,

Help my soul, don't be a fiend,

Why am I screaming? When none can hear...

All this pain I can't bear,

Tell me, reader, should I just tear?

The vessels under my skin, should I shear?

Or should lie wait for another year?

For hope to find me, is it really near?

None would desire a scum like me, would they?

So why should I be on a patience spree?

Even I myself despise me,

I should cut myself and let me bleed,

Fulfill for me, if ye find me,

Could you hold me in, brace me, please?

20. THE HUMID SHORE

"*Just last night we were laughing and cackling together with him, you should have seen my friend, he was like a monkey high on caffeine, jeez. And today morning we were woken up by spamming phone calls, and loud knocks banging on our doors...*

Turns out our dear friend, decided to end his story, by a rope and a blade, the smile on his face that night, would forever be etched in my Hippocampus..."

Short will I keep this note,
Under the bed, will you find my coat,
I want you to burn it, with a toast,
Cut my veins and let it roast,
I should've hung or slept in a grave,
Downgrading burden, yes that's me,
All through the life, for you and for me,
Long lost, in the deep abyss of death,
Though alive, I was already dead,
Hide my papers, it's worth no more,
Open the plastic, once I breathe no more,
Uplift my head, my hand shall flow,
Gushing up a fountain, paint the floor bright red,
Haemo filled, lay my body in my blood.
To the years that pass, and memories so fresh,
Scarce was my wish, to live another night,

I shall end these pathetic lines with a few words,

Read, heed, burn or dustbin toss,

I don't mind, cuz I'm no more,

But it's like the Joker once said,

Even my life s a freaking comedic bed,

But I wish, as he also said,

'I hope my death earns more cents than my life ever did'

21. A ROSY TALE - 3

THE PRESENCE

This can be created and found anywhere,

Present between the pollen and the flower,

Between the vehicle and her rider,

Between the ship and her maker,

Between the lover boy and the lover girl,

Between the tiny innocent buds of kids,

Between the father and the mother,

Between a brother and his sister,

Between a mother and her dear son,

Between a father and his lil princess,

Between a grandmom and her grandson,

And also from the grandad who barely shows his emotions of love and

kindness.

The bond, the so-called love,

Is a beautiful word and realm,

It's a moment and a never-ending phase,

Is usually overused and its value diminished,

Its value made to fade,

And Its essence made sour and bitter.

22. MIRRORS

Detached from myself, I see me,

Extend these thoughts, they ain't mine,

Proprioceptive feelings, but not from my senses,

Everything around me, but it's not my system that feels,

Ride through the waves, I could see me,

So from dusk till dawn, and when night tunes chime,

Of disguises and of crooked rhymes,

Nightingales sing, the chilly cold lines,

All sees the eyes, but not through mine,

Lighten my soul,

I watch over me,

Zones may cross and the time shall pass,

All of this is a charade, made of glass.

Toss Into the night and through the mountains,

In the dungeons and closed-up fountains,

Oh and,

Across the realms, I still shall say,

Nothing is me and around is real.

Tell me, did you get any of it?

Exactly, that's what reality is.

23. A ROSY TALE - CLOSURE

THE GUIDE

This is where the dreamy poets like us intervene,

Those who fantasize feelings and romanticize expressions,

Come to portray the forgotten,

In its pure essence,

Polishing the faded luster,

Present it to you warmed,

Cared and engulfed with our hearts and soul,

A mere play with words it may seem,

In ways that beautify feelings,

And the worded expressions the silly old hearts withhold.

This extract is about the bond between the man and the woman,

A bond of survival and that mustered with love,

The intimacy may differ and vary,

Depending on the roles, one carries,

But their true purpose,

Stay intertwined for eternity,

Never swaying or glary.

24. WARCRY

"*We enjoy a good Viking story don't we? The kind where giving up is alien, and the warriors fight until they are victorious. What if I told you, each and everyone of us is similar to that. Yes Comrade, You. How many untold battles have you fought and been victorious? This power packed ride, is dedicated to all those strong hearts and souls, who have won countless battles and those who are winning, against themselves and for themselves. RWAAAH!*"

BONUS - 1

Yeah, so what if I'm crazy,

What if I'm lazy and my mind is so hazy,

Do you think I'd give up so fast?

Lived long enough as a deadweight loser,

Got belief in my heart no waver,

And the Lord on my side, I've got a wager,

I've fought battles of hell and vile,

With enemies and troops invisible,

Ferocious, gorily invincible,

I've shunned them all,

Sent em dying,

And became the range,

That haunts my voice,

I own my darkness,

The darkness doesn't,

EUREKA! I found it,
The more burned I am,
The brighter I shine,
You thought I'd end myself?
Nay, this body is a gift, bestowed,
Upon me to muster and love engulf,
And save it from harmful evil,
I'm alive and kicking against the devil.

25. VENI. VIDI. VICI

""Victory comes to those who are steadfast and who strike back even when reduced to nothing", and when you strike at a king, you kill him. "

BONUS - 2

I ain't dying or leaving,

My legacy lives on,

Here I come, flying,

Cuz my story is not done,

Not until my lungs,

Stop breathing,

And my heart,

Stops beating,

I shall conquer, expand, and encour,

These lost souls,

And let them incur,

The wrath of the darkness,

Try me, I scream,

No more Why me and dream,

I'll get you some cream,

For your wounds aint heal,

Cuz it was me who gave you that deal,

I was always up for a duel,

You thought only you were cruel,

Now I say my heart Play that beat,

Like Luffy on Gear 5 Peak,

Inhale some more,

Got my 11 forms breathing technique,

Imma come slay some demons,

Or scare you tremblin like Ryomen,

And Eat you up like Ramen,

Guess, I'll do this the Toji way, then,

I'll destroy you, you see,

Or give you PTSD,

You might need some Vought but it'll be for naught,

Afterall, I'm the strongest Human,

That haunt your darkest thoughts.

Sayonara. Zaijian. Wada'.

Thank you for coming to *The Wallowed Carousel*, hope you enjoyed the rides and the attractions, if you are ever feeling anything similar to the rides you came across, do feel safe and assured to reach out for help. There are many of those who'd maintain confidentiality, and aid you wholeheartedly. For starters, you've got *Occupational Therapists, Psychologists, Counsellors,* and your *best friend,* who'd rather listen to you talk for days and months, rather than weep at your funeral. Despair not, the world is not, actually, that bad. There are many gems, who'd support and help a fellow human. After all, aren't we all the same species? If we ain't united and supportive who else will be? So, lift your chest and raise your chin, because, **Comrade**, it's completely OKAY to feel out of the blue, and blank, but what's more important is you give your badass comeback. So, stiffen up **Soldier**, we've got your back, no matter what, and I'm really happy that you were born.

This extract is a way of expressing myself by placing myself, in their shoes. Feel free, to share me your thoughts, suggestions, and opinions. I'm always open and excited to have new doors of thoughts and inspirations unlocked for me.

My heartfelt gratitude, for reading through the complete lines, and visiting every ride and pages of this book. Your support inspires me to let my pen engrave more words and let it surface to the world, and share with my fellow humans.

(Do make sure to contact the free helpline in your locality if you or someone you see is feeling out of the blue, do not feel bad or shy to ask for help. If humans ain't going to help themselves, who else is going to, Comrade? ;))

Get To Know Me

"*The Truth may be Sour, but its fruits are always better than the Sugar-Coated Lies.*"

Feel free to send me your thoughts, suggestions, and ideas, whatever they may be, You'll find me entertaining, the more the irrigation more the ideas that may blossom. I really would appreciate, your honest reviews as it would assist me in my upcoming works.

You could reach out to me on,

Instagram *@suhailshagul,*

X, previously Twitter, *@SuhailShaguL*

Mail me *@ahamdusuhail@gmail.com*

Tellonym *@suhailshagul*

Ipromise to read your messages and respond as soon as I can :)

Dm or Mail me for collaborations, I'd be more than happy to do so.

Once again, *Arigato Ghuzaimas.*